HAL LEONARD

OCARINA METHOD

BY CRIS GALE

To access video, visit:
www.halleonard.com/mylibrary

Enter Code
5342-8065-3944-6846

ISBN 978-1-4950-2514-3

7777 W. BLUEMOUND RD. P.O. BOX 13819 MILWAUKEE, WI 53213

In Australia Contact:
Hal Leonard Australia Pty. Ltd.
4 Lentara Court
Cheltenham, Victoria, 3192 Australia
Email: ausadmin@halleonard.com.au

Visit Hal Leonard Online at
www.halleonard.com

CONTENTS

INTRODUCTION

Welcome to the *Hal Leonard Ocarina Method*. Thank you for your interest in learning the ocarina. Following the method outlined in this book will arm you with the skills necessary to play the ocarina proficiently, as well as empower you to find and learn even more music. Because this book is for both beginners and musicians proficient at another instrument, the lessons start simple but become more involved as the book progresses. If a lesson gives you trouble, it is okay to go back and work on previous lessons. Practice leads to skill and, like all musical instruments, the ocarina takes practice. Also, remember that music should be fun. You don't have to practice 12 hours a day to become competent. Just try to set aside some time every day for a little practice, and you'll be playing well in no time.

In addition to the lessons, there is an appendix at the back of the book. The appendix includes a full chromatic fingering chart for 12-hole ocarinas, as well as a fingering chart for standard six-hole ocarinas. While this book is written for 12-hole ocarinas, much of it can be used for Italian-style ten-hole ocarinas and even some for four- or six-hole ocarinas. If you have purchased this book but have only a six-hole ocarina, you can use the six-hole fingering chart to work through many of the initial lessons. To get the most out of this method book, I recommend purchasing a good 12-hole ocarina. Because it is important to find a good instrument, I have included a buying guide on my website with ocarinas I recommend to my students (*http://CrisGale. com/Resources*). There you will also find my other ocarina resources, as well as information on ocarina gatherings and festivals.

Music is a lifelong endeavor, and in my opinion, the ocarina is the perfect choice. It has a beautiful tone, it is extremely portable, and it fits into many musical situations quite well.

Good luck and happy playing!

~ Cris Gale

A BRIEF HISTORY OF THE OCARINA

With ancient clay ocarinas discovered in meso-America, Central Africa, India, and China, and even instruments formed from animal horns in Europe, the ocarina is an instrument from all over the world. Independently developed by numerous cultures throughout its 12,000 years, the ocarina's history came to a focal point in Budrio, a tiny village in northern Italy. Where once the ocarina was limited to animal-shaped whistles and toys, in 1853 Giuseppe Donati created the first concert-tuned ocarina.

With the help of his apprentices, Donati's invention traveled all over the world. In the 1900s, it made its way to America and became known as the "Sweet Potato." Troops took ocarinas with them to WWI, and the U.S. government issued ocarinas to soldiers in WWII. In 1928, a Japanese craftsman named Takashi Aketagawa further improved the instrument by crafting 12-hole ocarinas capable of playing three more semitones. In 1960s England, John Taylor invented the pendant cross fingering system, creating an entirely new standard fingering system for the ocarina.

The current cultural resurgence of the ocarina can be traced back to a successful 1985 Japanese documentary called *The Great Yellow River*. Nomura Sojiro composed and performed the music for the film, which helped launch his career and inspired countless ocarina enthusiasts throughout Asia. Because of the ocarina's beautiful sound and popularity in Japan, Nintendo decided to incorporate it into their *Legend of Zelda* series of videogames, which in turn has inspired many new players around the world.

Like you, more and more people every day are choosing to learn the ocarina. The next chapter of the ocarina's history may very well be written by one of you.

▶ TYPES OF OCARINAS

Most ocarinas fall into one of two types: pendant and transverse.

Pendant ocarinas typically have a circular shape, and four to six finger holes. Within the pendant class, there are two subtypes: untuned pendants (pictured left) and English pendants (pictured right). An untuned pendant usually has finger holes that are all the same size, which makes them easy to identify. They are normally painted bright colors and are not suitable for most music. Often they are sold as souvenirs.

English pendant hole sizes vary. Conventionally, they play at least an octave of a diatonic scale. Many English pendants utilize relative tuning instead of concert tuning. Relative tuning means it is in tune with itself, but it's not ideal for playing with other instruments.

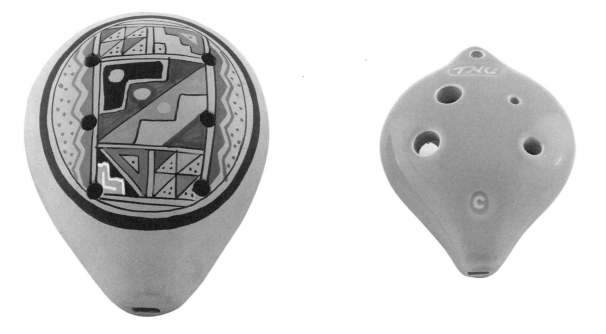

Transverse ocarinas ordinarily have a submarine-like shape and ten to 12 finger holes. Within the transverse class, there are two subtypes based on how the two highest notes are played. Italian-style transverse ocarinas (pictured left) typically have ten or 11 holes, with the highest note played with the right thumb. Asian-style transverse ocarinas (pictured right) commonly have 12 holes, with the highest note played with the left pinky. Both have linear fingering systems, are fully chromatic, and are regularly concert-tuned in C, G, or F. While the Asian style plays three additional semitones, they both have a range of approximately an octave and a half.

Pendant and transverse ocarinas also have multi-chamber varieties. A multi-chambered ocarina is a single ocarina that has multiple mouthpieces and chambers. It is like having two or more ocarinas in one.

Transverse multi-chambered ocarinas (pictured left) extend the range of a single-chambered transverse ocarina and continue the linear fingering system to each additional chamber. By adding a second and third chamber, the ocarina is capable of playing nearly three octaves for more complex and virtuosic music.

Pendant multi-chambered ocarinas (pictured right) use the English fingering system for each of the chambers, with those chambers normally tuned octaves, fourths, or fifths apart. This allows a single ocarinist to play counterpoint and harmony at the same time as the melody.

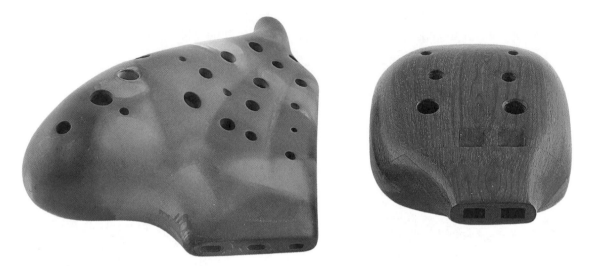

Ocarinas come in many different shapes, sizes, and tunings. Beginners sometimes have difficulty telling them apart. This book is written for 12-hole transverse ocarinas in C, but if you use the ocarina as a transposing instrument, 12-hole ocarinas in any tuning will work. In the Music Theory section, you will learn how to use the ocarina as a transposing instrument.

GETTING STARTED

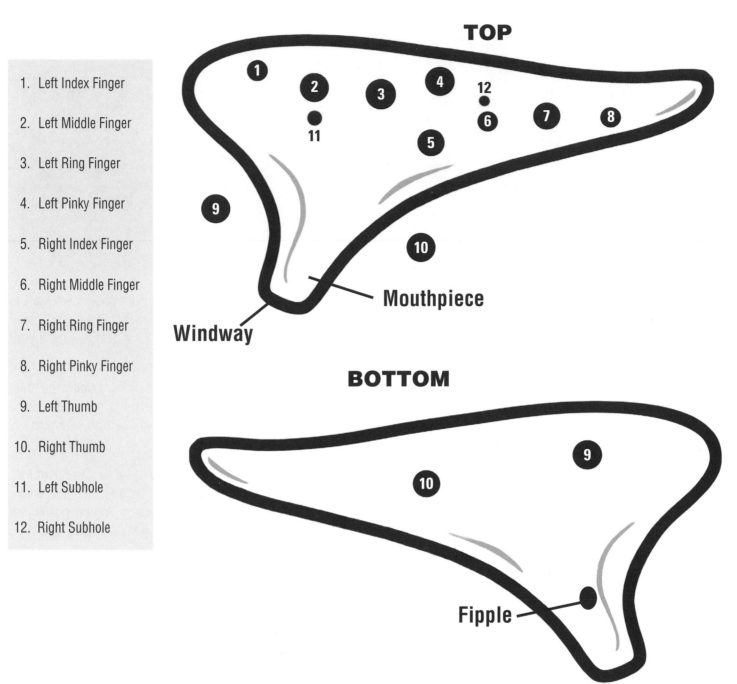

1. Left Index Finger
2. Left Middle Finger
3. Left Ring Finger
4. Left Pinky Finger
5. Right Index Finger
6. Right Middle Finger
7. Right Ring Finger
8. Right Pinky Finger
9. Left Thumb
10. Right Thumb
11. Left Subhole
12. Right Subhole

TOP

Mouthpiece

Windway

BOTTOM

Fipple

To hold the ocarina, you'll want to cover the ten main holes. There are eight on the top and two on the bottom. For now, leave the subholes uncovered. You have ten fingers, so let's start with covering just ten holes.

The diagram above has each hole numbered: 1–4 are for your left hand, and 5–8 are for your right hand. Your thumbs will cover the closest hole to each thumb on the bottom (that isn't the fipple). Now that you are holding the ocarina, your left palm should be facing you and your right palm should be pointed away from you.

Make sure you are keeping your fingers flat while you play, not using your fingertips (see the image below). Using the soft padded part of your fingers to cover the holes will give you a better seal. A better seal over the finger holes makes it much easier to stay in tune. If air is leaking from an unsealed hole, the note will be too high (sharp).

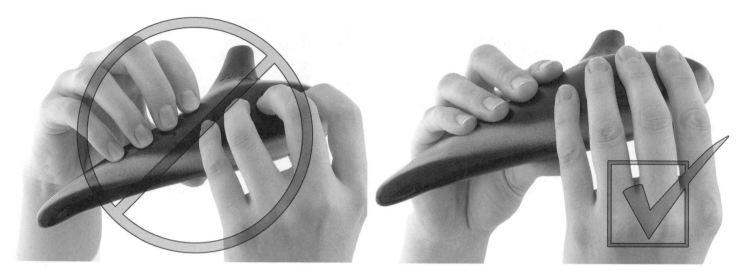

Many beginners grip the ocarina too tightly. You want to keep a firm but relaxed grip on the ocarina. Your fingers will start to ache quickly if you hold the ocarina too firmly. Playing the ocarina should not hurt, so if you are experiencing pain, you need to adjust your grip. If you aren't sure, practice over a soft surface as you find the right grip strength. As a general rule, if your finger pads have circular indentations after a practice session, you need to loosen your grip.

Getting a good seal takes practice. It is easy to shift your grip and find that you are not completely covering a hole. The most common culprits for leaking air are the thumbs, as well as the pinky and ring fingers. If a note sounds too sharp, check these fingers first to make sure they haven't rolled partially off the hole. Don't worry; as you become more familiar with your ocarina, your fingers will naturally acclimate to "home" position.

Compare your hand position with the photo above. Once your fingers are placed correctly, it is okay to make slight adjustments to your grip to seal the holes better and find a more comfortable position. Because finger length, hand size, and hand shape vary from person to person, it is important to take a moment to focus on how the ocarina feels in your hands, noting the position of each hole. In later lessons, you will learn to shift your hand position to stabilize the ocarina when playing the higher notes.

▶ MAKING YOUR FIRST SOUND

Before you blow into the ocarina, let's try an exercise that will teach you how to get a great sound out of the ocarina on your first try. Blowing into the ocarina has two components, breath and articulation. Your breath should be similar to blowing on a cup of hot cocoa. To articulate properly, whisper or say "too" at the beginning of the note. Now, put those skills together and blow into the mouthpiece. You should hear a strong start to the note, and if you blow consistently, the pitch will be steady. The pitch of the ocarina is governed by how hard you blow, so you'll have to practice keeping your breath steady. Also, you want to sit or stand up straight and try to keep your body in a natural yet comfortable alignment. Your back should be straight, and your neck and shoulders should be relaxed. If you are tense, try stretching your neck and shoulders to help relax them more. If you are standing, keep your knees slightly bent, with your weight evenly distributed between your feet. Good breathing technique begins with good posture.

Now that you can make a sound, let's discuss what is happening, and how to get the best sound possible. As you blow into the mouthpiece, a stream of air flows down the windway and meets the edge of the fipple, which makes the sound. When you inhale, you want to take nice, deep breaths that fill your lungs with lots of air. As you inhale, imagine your stomach is a balloon and fill it up. This will expand your diaphragm, which is important not only for having enough breath, but also later for vibrato. As you exhale, focus your lips and resist the urge to blow too hard. Your cheeks should not fill up, and your breath should be steady and consistent. Once you can make a sound, you can adjust your breath pressure to adjust your pitch.

▶ INTONATION

Now that you know how to hold the ocarina and make a sound, we can talk about being in tune. *Intonation* is a fancy word for "pitch accuracy." Playing in tune is important, to say the least. Because leaking air from the finger holes and changes in your airflow both affect pitch, intonation may be challenging at first. While practice will naturally develop muscle memory for covering the holes and improving breath control, it is also a good idea to work with a tuner at first to establish a better idea of the amount of breath needed to play each note in tune. Focusing on intonation now will begin training your ear immediately for what sounds right, and prevent you from having to unlearn bad habits later.

Technically, you cannot tune your ocarina as you can with many other instruments, but a tuner is still a good tool for a beginner to become more familiar with what I like to call the "breath slope" of your ocarina. Breath slope is the incremental increase of breath for each note as you go up the scale. A good ocarina will have a comfortable, intuitive breath slope. As a player, you may find your tastes change over time. For example, many beginners prefer softer breath ocarinas, but later discover that they enjoy higher breath ocarinas (with more back pressure) as their lung capacity increases. When practicing with a tuner, be sure to listen to the pitch while checking it against a tuner. You can also try to hold the note as long and as steady as possible. This will help with your intonation and breath control, and is also a way to increase your breath capacity.

If you do not have a tuner, you can tune with a digital piano or a tuning tone. In this case, you listen to the note played, and then try to match that note with your ocarina. When you are close, but not quite there, you'll feel a beating in your ears. If you make adjustments, you'll hear the tones match, and possibly even a ringing tone. Tuning to a reference pitch takes dedication and practice, though it can make playing with others much easier.

Cultivating both skills over time is important. A tuner will help you naturally play in concert pitch, while using a reference tone or using relative pitch can help you adjust your tuning to other instruments. Not all instruments stay perfectly in tune, though with practice, an ocarinist can adjust his or her intonation to match that of the other instruments.

 # MUSIC THEORY

The language of music is written as notes on a staff. The staff consists of five lines, with four spaces between the lines. The location of each note on the staff determines its pitch (highness or lowness). The higher the note is placed on the staff, the higher it sounds. A note with a deeper pitch appears lower on the staff. At the beginning of the staff is a clef sign. For the ocarina, we use the treble clef.

For notes that go above or below the treble clef, these notes are placed on ledger lines, which extend the music staff above and below.

Each line and space has a letter name. The lines are, from bottom to top, E-G-B-D-F. This is easy to remember as "Every Good Boy Does Fine." The spaces are, from bottom to top, F-A-C-E.

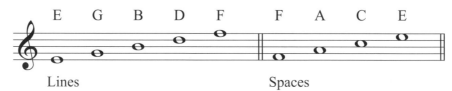

Your 12-hole ocarina will play a few of the notes on the lower ledger lines:

Music consists of notes or pitches that are set to a beat. This constant, steady pulse gives us a time value, which is also known as *rhythm*. The staff is divided by bar lines into units called measures or bars. A double bar is used to indicate a transition, or the end of a piece.

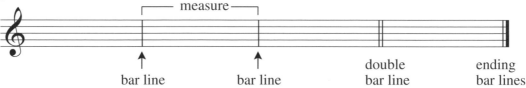

Each measure contains a specific number of beats, which is determined by the rhythm. When you tap your foot, for example, this is an expression of rhythm. The time signature, which is typically located next to the clef at the beginning of a piece of music, establishes the rhythm. It appears as two numbers. The top number indicates the number of beats in each measure. The bottom number tells us what kind of note gets one beat. You can remember this by asking "how many of what?" Here are some common time signatures:

$\frac{4}{4}$ = 4 beats per measure
= quarter note gets one beat

$\frac{3}{4}$ = 3 beats per measure
= quarter note gets one beat

$\frac{6}{8}$ = 6 beats per measure
= eighth note gets one beat

RHYTHM VALUES

Besides pitch, notes also indicate the duration, or how long the note lasts within a measure. Different types of notes have different durations.

<u>Notes</u>

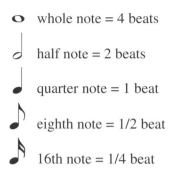

- o whole note = 4 beats
- ♩ half note = 2 beats
- ♩ quarter note = 1 beat
- ♪ eighth note = 1/2 beat
- ♬ 16th note = 1/4 beat

REST VALUES

A rest, or the silence between the notes, also has a duration, just like the notes. Their corresponding values are listed below.

<u>Rests</u>

- ▬ whole rest = 4 beats
- ▬ half rest = 2 beats
- 𝄽 quarter rest = 1 beat
- 𝄾 eighth rest = 1/2 beat
- 𝄿 16th rest = 1/4 beat

▶ TRANSPOSING INSTRUMENTS

This section will explain the methodology behind using the ocarina as a transposing instrument. Using the ocarina in this manner allows you to learn a single fingering system and apply it to every ocarina you play.

To put it simply, if you have a G ocarina and cover all the holes, your ocarina will make what we call "concert G." Rather than finding G on the staff and using that note, instead you will pretend your ocarina is in C, and read the sheet music as if it is in C. This means that even though you have a G ocarina, when you see a C, you will cover all the holes. After lesson 1, you will be able to play a piece in C on a C ocarina. If you want to play the same piece in G major, you only need to pick up a G ocarina and use the exact same fingering. The ocarina does the work for you.

Using a method book like this, you can easily transfer the skills and practice of playing a C ocarina on to any other tuning. In learning all the music of this book, you are learning it not only in the key that is written, but also can easily transpose it to any key, just by using a different ocarina.

If this is confusing, don't worry. As you learn more about the ocarina, this advantage will become apparent.

For now, let's focus on your first notes.

▶ C MAJOR SCALE: C, D, & E
(Playing Your First Notes)

We will start by learning the notes for the key of C major.

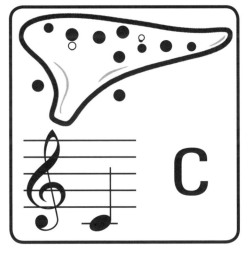

Make sure no air is leaking. Every hole should be covered, except for the subholes, which we will explore in a later lesson.

count
mentally: 1   2   3   4   1   2   3   4   1   2   3   4   1   2   3   4

Remember to make the "too" sound at the beginning of each note. Count along with the beat as you play each quarter note.

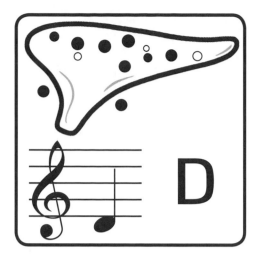

To play D, lift your right pinky. Don't lift it too high, since you want it to be ready to cover the hole again if you need to play C.

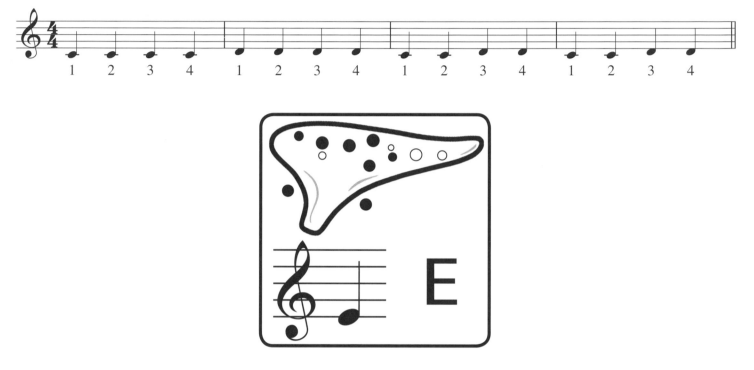

To play E, lift both your right pinky and right ring finger. Again, don't lift them too high.

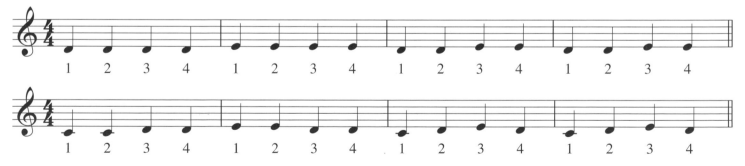

Now that you can play C, D, and E, let's incorporate some different types of notes. Half notes (♩) get two beats, so you will hold the note for that duration. For whole notes (𝅝), count four beats.

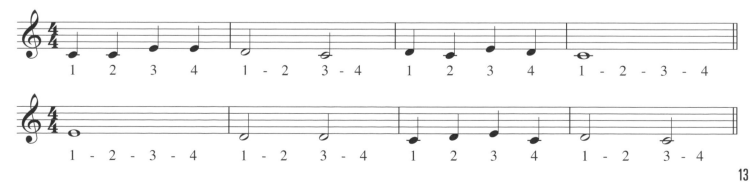

Now, let's play some familiar songs with the notes we've learned so far!

HOT CROSS BUNS

Traditional

MARY HAD A LITTLE LAMB

Traditional

▶ THE C MAJOR SCALE: F & G

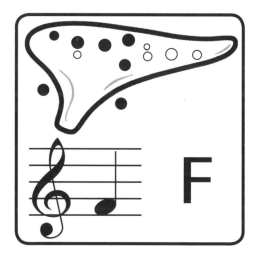

For F, all the fingers on your left hand, as well your right hand's thumb and index finger, should still be covering their respective holes. (Your right middle finger lifts for F and drops for E.)

Let's practice playing from E to F.

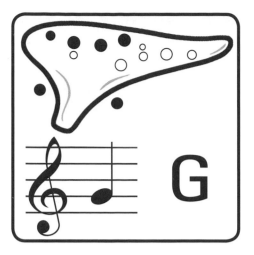

To play G, lift your right index finger. As each finger lifts for the next note, you may find it becomes easier to get the correct pitch, because there are fewer places for air to escape unintentionally. If the pitch is still wavering, it may be from changes in your breath pressure. Do your best to keep the airflow as steady as possible.

This etude will give you some practice playing from F to G.

Now we'll mix it up with all the notes and rhythms we know so far.

At first, lifting more than one finger at a time may take a little practice. Sometimes the pinky and ring finger seem to want to move independently when you need them to work together. In measure 3 of the exercise just above, make sure you play from E to C. (Your fingers may want to go to D instead.) Continue to count mentally with the rhythm for your quarter, half, and whole notes. Use a metronome to reinforce a steady beat.

Now that we can play C through G, we can perform another simple song. "Lightly Row" is a traditional 19th century German folksong.

LIGHTLY ROW

German Folksong

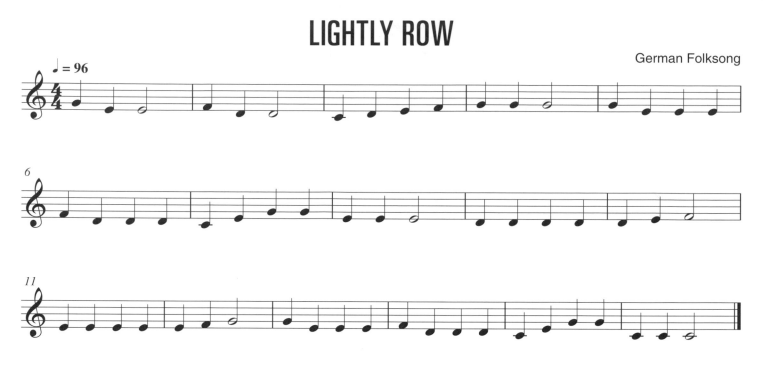

For the next piece, we'll need to learn about eighth notes. One quarter note is equal to two eighth notes. A single eighth has a flag. Multiple eighth notes are connected with a beam.

When we count eighth notes, we are measuring in halves of beats. An easy way to count them is to say "and" between each beat.

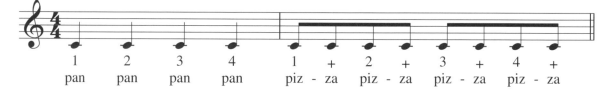

Even though measure 2 has twice as many notes, they take the same amount of time to play. The eighth notes are played twice as fast. If you are having difficulty counting the rhythm at first, try saying "pan" for every quarter note, and "pizza" for every pair of eighth notes.

Now try mixing quarter notes with eighth notes.

The example below incorporates the notes we've learned so far.

Make sure you hold the last note for the full four beats. It might help to tap your foot or use a metronome to make sure your beats are steady. Let's try some more exercises to continue practicing eighth notes.

You'll recognize this melody immediately: Beethoven's "Ode to Joy." Notice that it includes a few eighth notes.

ODE TO JOY

By Ludwig van Beethoven

▶ THE C MAJOR SCALE: A

Our next note is A. This is the first note that breaks the pattern of the linear fingering system. At first, it may feel strange lifting the left ring finger before the left pinky, but the left pinky will play an important role in maintaining balance on the highest notes later on. It will be the last finger you lift.

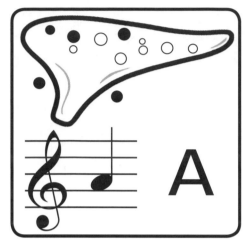

Here's an easy exercise that moves back and forth between G and A:

You may find that your left ring finger has a little trouble moving independently of your left pinky, just as your right ring and pinky did. If so, keep practicing and your fingers will figure it out. Also, you may need to adjust and loosen your grip slightly.

Using the notes and rhythms you already know, let's play several familiar tunes. Since the beat number is no longer written beneath the measures, count in your head or tap your foot to make sure your tempo is steady. Of course, a metronome will work, too!

TWINKLE, TWINKLE LITTLE STAR

Traditional

♩ = 104-108

18

In measures 6 and 8, remember to keep your left pinky down. It should stay firmly planted. (If necessary, review the G-to-A exercise.) With more practice, your muscle memory will eventually kick in, and it will feel more natural to play A.

GO TELL AUNT RHODY

Traditional

In "Long Long Ago," measure 2 is a group of notes that recurs in measures 6 and 14. Be sure you are making smooth transitions from the G to the E, so your right index and middle fingers are working together to cover the holes at the same moment.

LONG LONG AGO

By Thomas Bayly

Before playing "Frère Jacques" in its entirety, practice measure 5. Since you need to lift and drop your left ring finger quickly for the eighth notes, make certain you are getting a good seal over the left ring finger hole for G and also that you are lifting it off completely for A.

FRÈRE JACQUES

French Folksong

Practice Spot: A practice spot is a group of notes (or measures) you isolate and practice independently of the rest of the piece, as you did with measure 5 in "Frère Jacques." Playing some extra repetitions of the trouble spots will make the most of your practice. When you go back to playing the whole exercise or song again, you'll find it is not difficult. It is important to continue working on a practice spot after playing it correctly for the first time. Several more repetitions after you play it correctly will reinforce the skill or technique, making it easier to apply the concept to similar situations.

We'll identify good places for practice spots, because approaching music in this manner will set you up for success in the long run.

 # DOTTED RHYTHM

Let's start learning about dotted rhythms. We'll begin with the dotted-half note. When you add a dot to a note, you add half of the beat value. A regular half note has two beats and the dot adds one more beat, so a dotted-half note is held for three beats.

On page 10, we mentioned 3/4 time. You'll notice the following exercise has a 3/4 time signature. Since there are three beats per measure, this rhythm works well and is easy to count.

The curved line connecting the C in measures 7 and 8 is called a tie. Since a tie connects two notes of the same pitch, even across a bar line, you should combine the beats and play it as a single note. In this case, you would start playing the C in measure 7, and hold it for six beats. Make sure you take a deep breath so you don't run out of air.

At the end of measure 6 there is a breath mark. Any time you need to remember to take a breath, mark this symbol as a reminder. Use a pencil with an eraser, since where you breathe may change depending on how fast you play, or as your lung capacity increases.

Try playing dotted-half notes again in common time, a time signature that is another name for 4/4. It is notated with a large "C."

Each measure gets four beats. Be sure to count along, either by tapping your foot or with the help of a metronome. Make certain the dotted-half note is held for three full beats before you play the quarter note.

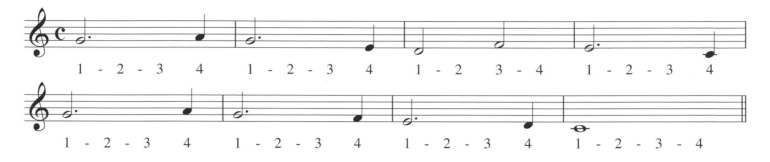

1 - 2 - 3   4   1 - 2 - 3   4   1 - 2   3 - 4   1 - 2 - 3   4

1 - 2 - 3   4   1 - 2 - 3   4   1 - 2 - 3   4   1 - 2 - 3 - 4

Stephen Foster (1826–1864) was America's first great songwriter. His melodies are so much a part of our history and culture that most people think they're folk tunes. "Oh! Susanna" is no exception. Let's use its familiar melody to practice playing the dotted-half note.

OH! SUSANNA

By Stephen Foster

Now we move on to the dotted-quarter note. A regular quarter note is held for one beat. Since the dot adds half of the beat value, you add half of a beat. A dotted-quarter note is held for one-and-a-half beats.

Another way of looking at it, which may help with counting the rhythm, is to think of the dotted-quarter note as three eighth notes.

In the same way that eighth notes are often grouped in pairs of two or four, dotted-quarter notes are often paired with an eighth note to complete the beat. You can count them the same way you count eighth notes.

1 + 2 +   1 + 2 +

The following easy exercise uses dotted-quarter notes and eighth notes. Since we are playing only G, focus on the counting, the rhythm, and start with a slower tempo.

1 + 2 + 3 + 4 +   1 + 2 + 3 + 4 +   1 + 2 + 3 + 4 +   1 + 2 + 3 + 4 +

Test your skill with another one. This time, the dotted-quarter note will start in the middle of the first beat, so instead of counting "1 and 2" you count "and 2 and," but it is still held for the same amount of time.

1 + 2 + 3 + 4 +   1 + 2 + 3 + 4 +   1 + 2 + 3 + 4 +   1 + 2 + 3 + 4 +

Dotted rhythms can be a bit tricky at first, so let's keep practicing!

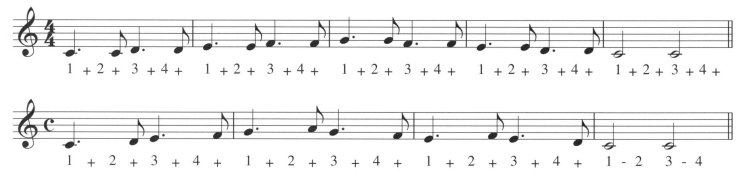

1 + 2 + 3 + 4 +   1 + 2 + 3 + 4 +   1 + 2 + 3 + 4 +   1 + 2 + 3 + 4 +   1 + 2 + 3 + 4 +

1 + 2 + 3 + 4 +   1 + 2 + 3 + 4 +   1 + 2 + 3 + 4 +   1 - 2   3 - 4

For this next exercise, it may take a moment for you to identify the eighth notes. Be sure to slow the tempo to a comfortable speed so you can play the rhythm correctly.

1 + 2 + 3 + 4 +   1 + 2 + 3 + 4 +   1 + 2 + 3 + 4 +   1 + 2 + 3 + 4 +   1 - 2 - 3 - 4

Let's try an exercise that incorporates more of the other rhythms we've learned so far.

1 + 2 + 3 + 4 +   1 + 2 + 3 + 4 +   1 + 2 + 3 + 4 +   1 + 2 + 3 + 4 +

Now that you're more familiar with dotted rhythms, have another go at "Oh! Susanna." This time, several pairs of dotted-quarter notes and eighth notes have replaced the regular quarter notes. Measures 1, 2, 5, and 6 are great places for practice spots. Be certain you are playing the dotted rhythms correctly.

OH! SUSANNA

By Stephen Foster

The next few tunes will reinforce your understanding of dotted rhythms. Remember to isolate your problem measures. It's okay to review previous exercises if necessary.

LONDON BRIDGE

Traditional

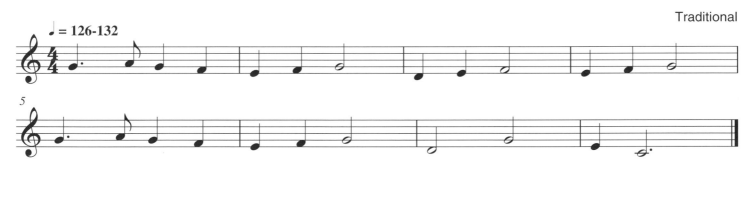

KUMBAYA

Congan Folksong

MY BONNIE LIES OVER THE OCEAN

Traditional

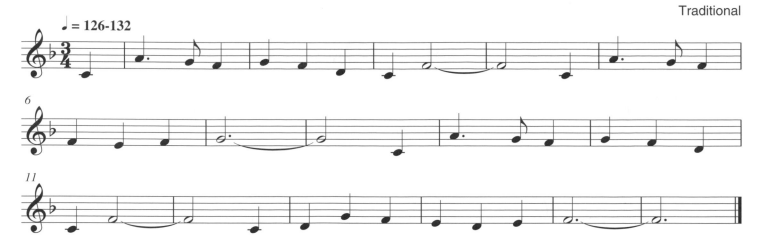

Make sure you play the notes with ties for the combined lengths of the notes. Add a breath mark at the end of measure 14 to help you remember.

THE C MAJOR SCALE: B & C

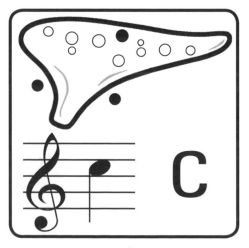

To play B, you'll need to raise the left middle finger. Make sure your left pinky doesn't lift yet.

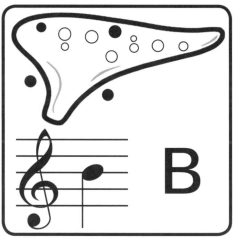

For C, lift your left index finger. Now the ocarina is balanced on your thumbs with the left pinky acting as a counterbalance. Take a moment to study the position of the new notes on the staff of the treble clef.

Always practice with a tuner when you learn new notes. You may notice that you need to blow a little harder to play B and C in tune.

Have a go at this simple etude, playing A and B.

Now we'll practice B and C.

Adding a little complexity, this exercise covers A, B, and C and uses dotted rhythms.

Now that you can play a whole octave in C major, from low C to high C, we'll attempt a few exercises that use all the notes you've learned so far. The first employs the C major scale. As you play, make sure you are counting the rhythms correctly. If a measure gives you trouble, go back to the exercises to review that specific rhythm.

Here you'll find both arpeggios and stepwise motion. Listen for accurate rhythm and clear intonation.

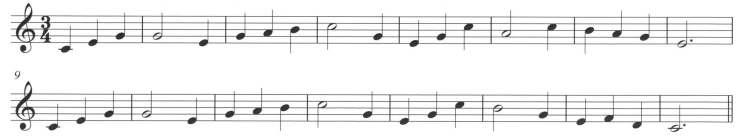

If you find that you are having trouble identifying notes quickly enough to play the rhythm correctly, try slowing the tempo and reviewing exercises earlier in this book. It might also be helpful to use flash cards. The faster you can identify the notes, the easier it is to play the rhythm correctly.

Let's learn some new songs!

VIVA LA FRANCE

French Folksong

In "Row, Row, Row Your Boat," you see a quarter rest in measure 8. This means you are silent for one beat. In music, silence is just as important as the notes. Use a metronome, count the beats, or tap your foot to help you keep the rhythm. (If you need to, refer back to page 11.)

ROW, ROW, ROW YOUR BOAT

Traditional

"Lullaby of Takeda" is a lovely folk melody from Japan. Watch for the ties and quarter rests as you play measures 7 and 8.

LULLABY OF TAKEDA

Japanese Folksong

As we continue to make use of our new notes, let's review dotted rhythms.

MAY SONG

Traditional

LULLABY
(Cradle Song)

By Johannes Brahms

Slurs sometimes look a lot like ties, but they are used to connect notes that are different pitches. A tie is played as one long note, but to play a slur, we do something different. All the notes within the curved line should be played as a single phrase, which means you should articulate only the first note with a "too" sound. If you avoid tonguing the other notes, it will give them a smoother, more fluid phrasing called legato.

Using slurs, let's play a C major scale with legato phrasing. For measure 1, you tongue the C, and you lift your right pinky without tonguing the D to give it legato articulation. When you get to measure 5, you should tongue the C. Avoid tonguing D, E, and F. The next note you should tongue is the G.

Now that you can play slurs, let's take a crack at Brahms's "Lullaby" again, with more legato phrasing this time.

LULLABY
(Cradle Song)

By Johannes Brahms

If you enjoy playing beautiful melodies, I recommend experimenting with legato phrasing. Phrasing is an important part of musical interpretation that can add a lot to your performance and help you develop your own unique playing style.

▶ THE C MAJOR SCALE: D
(Using Support Fingers)

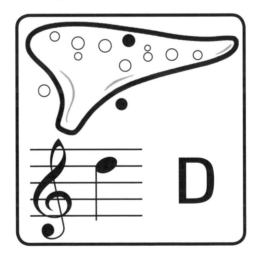

To play D, the next finger up is the left thumb. If you try to lift this finger, it becomes difficult to support the ocarina safely on only two fingers. In order to play the remaining notes, it will be necessary to change your hand position. Fortunately, there are a few techniques that will make it easier to play the highest notes. The correct technique will depend on the situation, and what feels comfortable for your hands. Let's talk about *support fingers*.

Using support fingers involves repurposing some of your fingers that are already lifted off the finger holes to help stabilize the tail or side of the ocarina so your remaining fingers (the thumbs and left pinky) can lift without losing your balance or grip on the ocarina.

You can use your right pinky as a counterbalance, with most of the weight of the ocarina resting on your right thumb. Take care to place your pinky on the tail of the ocarina without covering any of the finger holes. (That would lower the pitch.) Most likely, muscle memory will kick in, and your fingers will want to go to the "home" position. Resist the urge, making sure your pinky is extended a bit farther than the finger hole. Let's practice using this technique to play up to D.

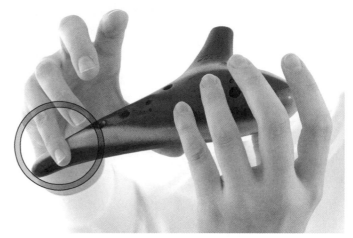

To achieve a smooth transition, anticipate the shifting balance point before you get to high D. At some point between G and C, you want to drop your support finger; this will allow you to play the D easily without interrupting the rhythm. The more you practice, the more it becomes second nature; eventually it will become a graceful, flowing motion that feels unified. Practice this exercise again a few times. Your support finger should drop in measure 2 whenever it feels comfortable for you, and it should lift again in measure 4 as soon as it feels natural to lift it. This way, the ocarina stays properly supported at all times.

I recommend using just the pinky as a support finger for fast, intricate music. Using this technique, you will be able to play the remaining high notes above D by rolling the thumbs and left pinky off the holes. You can move faster between high notes and low notes without having to change your hand position as much, but phrasing may be a bit trickier.

A different technique for supporting the ocarina on the highest notes involves using both your right ring and pinky fingers to grip the tail of the ocarina. Using this method, these two fingers will support most of the weight of the ocarina, with other support fingers acting as a counterbalance later on. Since you want to avoid covering any finger holes with your support fingers, this technique works better on ocarinas with longer tails. If your ocarina has more of a round shape, the previous technique may be a better choice, or another one we'll discuss soon. By gripping the tail of the ocarina with two fingers, it creates enough stability for the remaining fingers to be able to lift off instead of roll off. You may notice the ocarina feels more balanced and secure in your hands with this technique.

Using this technique, play the exercise again. Drop your support fingers whenever you like in measure 2, and lift them again in measure 4. Since it may take a little more effort to change your hand position, try to anticipate the shift, and make the transition as smooth as possible without disrupting the rhythm.

A bit more practice may be required for this technique to become smooth as you transition up to D. This technique is ideal for slower melodies, because being able to lift the remaining fingers lends itself to better, more precise phrasing. On the other hand, it may not be the best technique when you need to transition quickly between high notes and low notes. As you learn more music, you'll encounter a variety of situations. I recommend practicing and becoming familiar with more than one technique so you can discover what works best for you, or for that situation. With more practice, you may find that one technique is a better fit for your hands, your playing style, or even the shape of your ocarina.

Here are a few more exercises to practice using support fingers. For the first two, you can use the arrows as a guide for when to drop or lift your support fingers, and give it a go with both techniques.

Keep in mind: the arrows are just suggestions. You can decide to drop or lift support fingers whenever it feels natural to help keep the ocarina balanced in your hands.

For the next exercise, use your own judgment for the timing as you place and lift your support fingers.

Resist the urge to mark the arrows on the page; give your support fingers a chance to drop when it feels natural for them now. If necessary, repeat the exercises a few more times until the technique becomes more familiar. As your fingers develop muscle memory, using support fingers becomes second nature.

Now that you've practiced using support fingers, put the new technique to use on a popular song. For measure 3, you definitely want to use support fingers for the high D. In other places, like measures 14–16, support fingers are optional for C, A, and G. In these instances, experiment and see what works best for you. Plan accordingly to make sure you don't run out of breath for the notes with the ties. Breath marks always help!

MORNING HAS BROKEN

Gaelic Melody

"Scarborough Fair" is a traditional English ballad that goes back several centuries. In the 1960s, Simon and Garfunkel added a countermelody and new lyrics to create "Scarborough Fair/Canticle."

SCARBOROUGH FAIR

Traditional English Ballad

Let's add another Stephen Foster melody to our growing repertoire. In "Swanee River," support fingers are necessary for the high D in measure 9. You could start using them at the beginning of measure 9, all the way until the F in measure 11. It is optional for the notes that are not D, but using them throughout this phrase provides support without being overly disruptive to your rhythm and phrasing. Support fingers are also optional in measures 2, 6, and 14, but I find that my support fingers seem eager to spring into action when I leap more than a few steps from a lower note to a higher note. This is a good habit, since it lowers the risk of dropping your ocarina.

SWANEE RIVER

By Stephen Foster

Now that you are more familiar with a couple of techniques for using support fingers, we can approach the remaining high notes.

▶️ THE C MAJOR SCALE: E & F
(Playing the Highest Notes)

The highest notes require more breath than the lower notes. This is especially true for E and F. If the note doesn't sound clear, make sure you are using enough breath; focus your breath by tightening your lips slightly to increase the pressure of the air through the windway. Be certain the windway is clear of condensation.

To remove condensation from the windway, cover the fipple with your thumb and blow a quick blast of air through the mouthpiece. This will force the condensation out and allow those notes to sound clear.

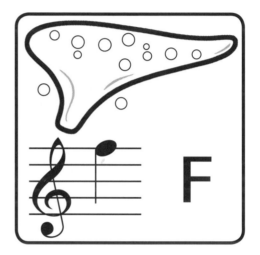

When you played high D, you lifted your left thumb. Let's talk about where to place it when playing high E and F. This technique coincides with using two support fingers.

If your ocarina is made of ceramic, I highly recommend practicing these techniques over a soft surface until you get the hang of them.

For D, the thumb lifts, and if you don't need to go any higher, you don't need to change your hand position. To go higher, your left thumb becomes the next support finger by moving to the left side (or nose) of the ocarina. Depending on the shape of your ocarina, you can place it anywhere between the left thumb hole and the side of the ocarina that provides the best balance and support.

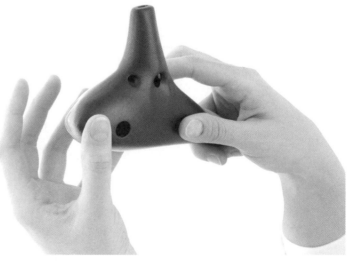

While most of the weight of the ocarina is supported by the right ring and pinky finger, the left thumb acts as a counterbalance. If you remove the left thumb, the ocarina should still be supported, but the left thumb provides extra stability. With your ocarina properly supported, now your right thumb and left pinky can lift off the holes so you can play high E and F.

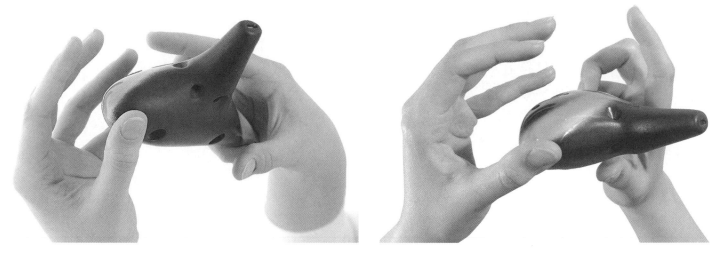

To get the best sound, you need to use more breath support. You can also enhance the tone slightly by leaning forward.

Make sure the support fingers on your right hand are gripping the tail of the ocarina in a way that allows your right thumb to rest in a comfortable position when it is covering the right thumb hole. Your right thumb should be able to extend straight and cover the hole with the fleshy part of your finger pad. Just like your other fingers, the fingertip won't seal the hole as well, so if your thumb is either bent or stretched, you'll want to adjust your grip.

Start by covering the right thumb hole with the pad of your finger, then place the right ring and pinky support fingers on the tail of the ocarina based on where your thumb is comfortable, taking care not to cover any finger holes on the tail of the ocarina.

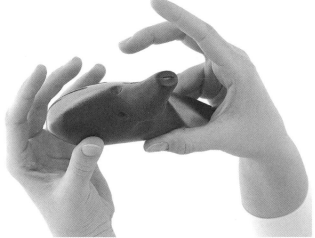

A variation of this technique is to press the tail of the ocarina into your right palm. Your left thumb supports the nose of the ocarina, and your right ring and pinky fingers wrap around the front of the ocarina, being careful not to cover the finger holes.

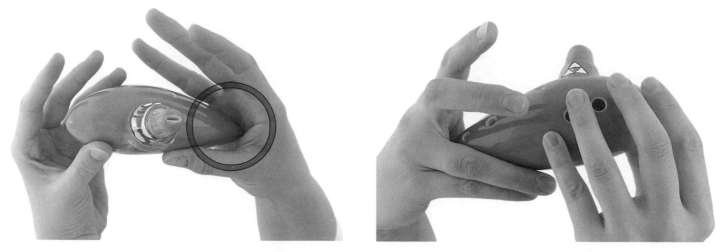

If your ocarina has more of a round shape, or if there isn't a lot of space beyond the pinky hole on the tail of the ocarina, this hand position might work better for you so that you don't accidentally cover a hole, which will lower the pitch. Leaning forward provides the best balance and support in this situation. It will also give your high notes more clarity.

Again, these techniques are ideal for slower melodies, because changing your hand position constantly for faster music can be difficult. These techniques give you more flexibility for phrasing and **ornamentation**, especially for transitioning smoothly between the high notes: for example, playing from D to E, or E to F.

Ornamentation: fast notes around a central note that are not necessary for the melody, but are used to decorate or embellish the melody

Let's look at how to play high E and F if you use only the pinky as a support finger. Since your hand position does not need to change as much, this technique works great for fast music, and in situations where you need to transition quickly back and forth between high notes and low notes. Your thumbs and left pinky will be used to balance the ocarina at all times; instead of lifting off the holes, they will roll off. The right pinky support finger doesn't bear the weight of the ocarina, it just provides a little extra support as a counterbalance.

Starting with C, the ocarina is balanced between the thumbs and left pinky, with the right pinky acting as a support finger.

To play D, the left thumb rolls off the hole.

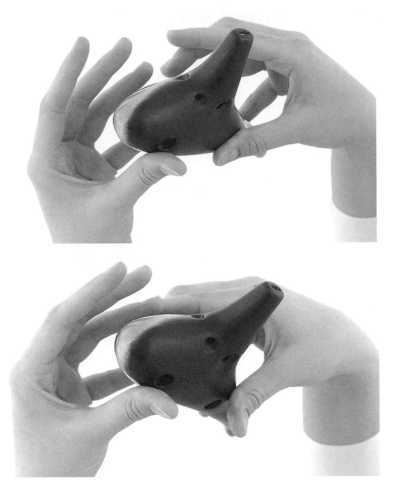

To play E, the right thumb can roll backward just like the left thumb.

Alternatively, you can also roll it the other way and use the right index finger as an extra support finger to brace the top of the ocarina alongside the mouthpiece.

I use both techniques, but the second has the added benefit of being able to lift the left thumb for D. If you use the right index finger for support, make sure that it doesn't cover any finger hole.

For F, the left pinky rolls back in both cases. With all the holes uncovered, the balance has shifted slightly from the pads of the fingers to the area closer to the first knuckle.

I mentioned earlier that phrasing is more difficult with this technique. If you are not fast and precise when you roll your thumbs and left pinky, the note will sound like a pitch bend. Done intentionally, pitch bending can add style to your playing, but unintentionally, it can make your phrasing sound sloppy.

Pitch bend: a type of music ornament wherein the pitch slides to the next note instead of stepping cleanly to the next note

As you continue to learn more music, you'll choose the techniques that work best for the music you enjoy playing. Being familiar with different techniques will allow you to have the best tool for the job as you make these discoveries.

For the next set of exercises, use more than one technique. Try changing your hand position and lifting each finger; also, try rolling off the thumbs and left pinky. See what works best and feels the most comfortable for your hands. Don't forget to use increased breath on high E and F.

Let's continue to practice these techniques with some new music that incorporates the highest notes. Remember to count two beats of silence in measure 14 of "Pop Goes the Weasel."

POP GOES THE WEASEL

Traditional

YANKEE DOODLE

Traditional

"Pining for the Spring Breeze" is a lovely melody composed by Teng Yu-hsien, who is considered the father of Taiwanese folksongs.

PINING FOR THE SPRING BREEZE

By Teng Yu-hsien

Czech composer Antonin Dvořák (1841–1904) composed this beautiful melody for the slow movement of his "New World" Symphony. Play it with all the expressivity you can muster.

GOING HOME

By Antonín Dvořák

▶ DOTTED-EIGHTH NOTES

Let's set our sights on a new rhythm. You've had plenty of practice playing dotted-quarter notes, so now we turn our attention to dotted-eighth notes and 16th notes. Just like half notes and quarter notes, the dot adds half of the beat value. Since a regular eighth note is held for half of a beat, the dot adds a quarter of a beat, so a dotted-eighth note is held for three-fourths of a beat. A 16th note is held for one-fourth of a beat, so a dotted-eighth note is like adding a 16th note to an eighth note.

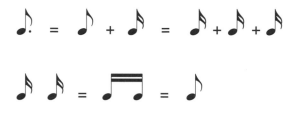

In the same way that dotted-quarter notes are frequently paired with eighth notes to complete the second or fourth beat in a measure, you will often see a dotted-eighth note paired with a 16th note, which equals one beat. All these note combinations equal one beat.

Since we're measuring in quarters of beats now, I recommend counting your beats in a slightly different way when you have 16th notes.

You can count the dotted-eighth and 16th notes in the same way, saying "one ee and ah," "two ee and ah," and so on, which divides each beat into four parts. Be sure to listen to the DVD for the next exercises, since it may be a little more difficult to count correctly for this new rhythm.

Let's practice the new rhythm using F and G.

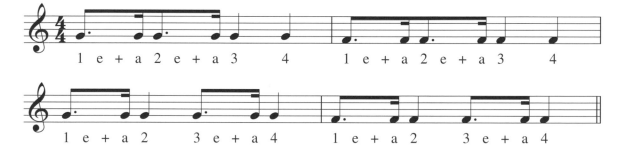

As you are counting, be sure to use "one ee and ah," "two ee and ah," "three ee and ah," "four ee and ah" now. Play the dotted-eighth note for "one ee and" and the 16th note for "ah." It will sound like a long note and short note. Let's practice it again using more of the ocarina's range.

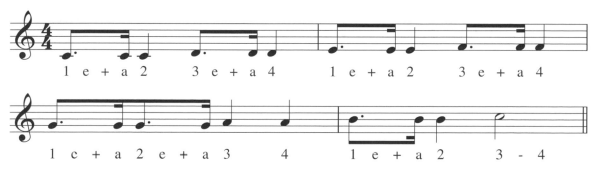

Focus on keeping the beat as steady as possible, either by counting, tapping your foot, or using a metronome at a comfortable speed.

Be sure to use the same rhythm for this next exercise. If you find you need to pause between the dotted-eighth note and the 16th note, try slowing the tempo so you can play the rhythm correctly.

Lend your best endeavor to one more.

Keep the tempo nice and steady, and don't hesitate to slow down if it makes it easier to play the rhythm correctly.

Time for new music!

COUNTRY GARDENS

English Folksong

Continue practicing dotted-eighth rhythms with "Humoresque," another famous piece by Antonin Dvořák. Measure 7 is a good place to make a practice spot, since you need to play quickly from a high C to a low C between the dotted-eighth and 16th note.

HUMORESQUE

By Antonín Dvořák

▶ PLAYING IN F MAJOR

Up to this point, we've focused on learning the C major scale and playing music that uses those notes. To play in F major, we need to learn a new note. In this key, B is flat, or slightly lower in pitch. We will play B♭ instead of B♮.

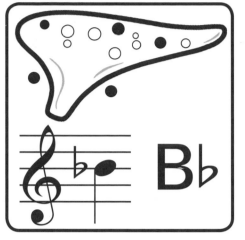

If you see this symbol (♭) next to a note, it means that the note is to be lowered a half step. This symbol may also appear in the key signature. For example, if a piece is in F major, the key signature will have the symbol on the B position. This lets you know the note should be played as B♭ instead of B (sometimes called B "natural" or B♮), even though the symbol is not next to the note itself.

Also, if you see the (♭) symbol next to a note, the symbol applies to all notes of that pitch until the next measure.

Practice playing from A to B♭.

Be sure your left middle finger is lifting at the same moment your right ring finger is dropping, and vice versa. It may take a little practice to get your fingers coordinated and working together smoothly. Don't forget that the flat symbol (♭) applies to each B, because it is in the same measure.

Practice playing from B♭ to C.

As you play from B♭ to C, make certain your left index finger and right ring finger are lifting and dropping together smoothly.

Are you ready to attempt the F major scale? (Of course you are!) This time, the flat symbol (♭) is in the key signature, so even though it doesn't appear next to each B, be vigilant about playing B♭ instead of B♮.

Did you notice that the F major scale sounds similar to the C major scale? Indeed, though it starts and ends on F instead of C.

Let's play new music in F major now.

"Furusato" is a beautiful melody from Japan that was written as a children's song. It means "Hometown."

FURUSATO

Japanese Folksong

FOR HE'S A JOLLY GOOD FELLOW

Traditional

Originally a folksong sung by Polish immigrants in America, "Westphalia Waltz" was later made famous by a Cotton Collins, a Texas fiddler. In the measures where you play high F, anticipate these phrases by placing your support fingers. Measure 10 has a tricky transition from B♭ to high F. Isolate these two notes and repeat them so you can decide which technique will give you the smoothest phrasing. You can roll the thumbs off the holes, or you can use more support fingers and lift the remaining fingers.

WESTPHALIA WALTZ

Based on a Polish Folksong

Now that we've played several songs in F major, let's learn some music in a minor key.

# PLAYING IN D MINOR

The D minor scale works well on your C ocarina. It uses the same notes as the F major scale, so again you will play Bb instead of B♮. The key signature looks the same, with the flat symbol (♭) on the B line.

Play a D minor scale.

You may notice that the D minor scale has a sad sound compared with the F major scale, even though it uses the same notes. You can listen for clues like this to help you identify whether a piece of music is in a major key or a minor key.

Let's play a couple of tunes in D minor.

"Korobeiniki" is a famous Russian folksong that is also well-known in pop culture. In measure 5, there's an eighth rest. This indicates half-a-beat of silence. The rhythm may be a bit tricky here, because the quarter note starts on the "and" of the first beat. Listen to the audio track a few times to get a sense of how the rhythm works.

KOROBEINIKI

Russian Folksong

This song is typically repeated. The repeat sign at the end lets you know to go back to the beginning.

repeat sign

"Drive the Cold Winter Away" is a traditional English carol. Before you try playing this D minor piece, practice playing measures 3 and 4, especially the transition from A to high F. Experiment and use the technique that gives you the best result. Also practice the transition in measure 12 from the high F to the low F, and in measures 22–23 from low D to high F. In each case, remember that the lower notes require softer breath and the higher notes require firmer breath to play in tune and get a good sound.

DRIVE THE COLD WINTER AWAY

Traditional English Carol

▶ PLAYING IN G MAJOR

G major is another key that works well for your C ocarina. To play music in G major, you need to learn only one new note: For this key, you'll need an F♯.

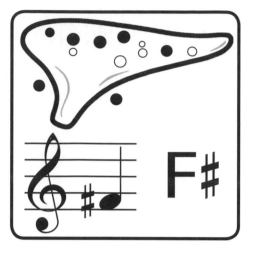

If you see the sharp symbol (♯) next to a note, it means that the note is to be raised a half step. If a piece is in G major, this symbol will appear in the key signature on the top line (F) of the treble staff; instead of playing F♮, we play F♯.

Just like the flat symbol (♭), a sharp symbol (♯) next to a note applies to all notes of that pitch until the next measure.

Practice playing from E to F♯.

When playing an F♯, two fingers are lifting at the same time as one is dropping; for that reason, you may find this note slightly difficult at first. Your right ring finger will be used for many of the other sharps and flats you will learn; it just takes some time and practice to develop the muscle memory for that finger. For F♯, try to focus on getting your right index, middle, and ring fingers to work together for a smooth transition.

Now practice playing from F♯ to G.

Playing from F♯ to G is much easier, since it only involves lifting and dropping the right ring finger.

Let's try playing a G major scale. This time, the sharp symbol (♯) is in the key signature rather than directly ahead of the note. In this case, we are limited by the range of the ocarina, since your highest note is F. However, you can still play a lot of music in G major.

Let's learn some new music.

"Aura Lee" is an American folksong with a melody you may recognize. See how long it takes you to guess it!

AURA LEE

American Folksong

Did you figure it out? Elvis Presley borrowed this folk tune for his song "Love Me Tender."

AULD LANG SYNE

Traditional Scottish Melody

DAISY BELL
(A BICYCLE BUILT FOR TWO)

By Harry Dacre

MUSETTE

By Johann Sebastian Bach

# PLAYING IN E MINOR

E minor is another popular key that works well for the C ocarina. It uses the same notes as G major, so F♯ will appear in the key signature; you should play an F♯ rather than an F♮.

Practice the E minor scale.

Let's learn a song in E minor.

GOD REST YE MERRY, GENTLEMEN

Traditional English Carol

♩ = 144

WE GOT RHYTHM

Make a brief review of dotted-eighth/16th rhythm. At the same time, we can practice 16th notes again with a new rhythm. Counting with "one ee and ah" and so on, we can play:

When you pair a regular eighth note with two 16th notes, it still adds up to one beat. You can use the words "salt pepper" or "soft kitty" to practice this rhythm.

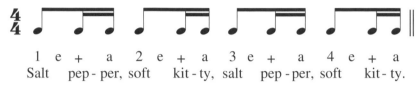

Practice the new rhythm.

We'll continue as before, but now there are some dotted-eighth notes mixed in. Make sure you are counting the rhythm correctly. You can review earlier exercises for more practice with dotted-eighth notes.

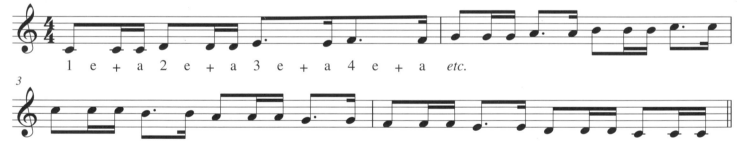

Okay, just one more. Now quarter notes and eighth notes are mixed in as well. Don't forget that quarter notes get a whole beat, or in this case, "one ee and ah."

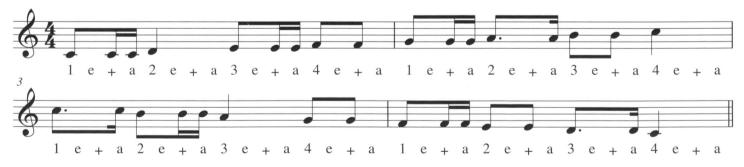

There's an old American sea chantey – "What Shall We Do with the Drunken Sailor?" – that uses all these rhythms. Try your hand at playing it now.

WHAT SHALL WE DO WITH THE DRUNKEN SAILOR?

American Sea Chantey

⏵ USING THE SUBHOLES: B, B♭, & A

The lowest notes on your ocarina are played by covering the subholes. If your ocarina does not have subholes, you can skip this section. If your ocarina has one subhole, you will be able to learn the next note.

The highest notes require extra breath to get the best sound. For the lowest notes, though, will need to develop good breath control to blow more gently, because the subhole notes require lighter airflow. It's important to make sure you are completely covering all the holes, since there are more places for air to leak unintentionally.

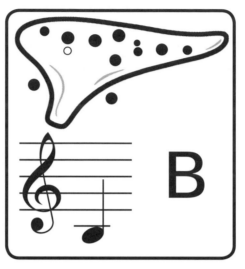

To play low B, slide your right middle finger until it covers both holes. Be patient with yourself. This usually takes some practice to get used to.

This exercise alternates low B and middle C.

If your finger is having difficulty sliding, make sure your grip is not too tight. Check that your finger is completely sealing both holes, since stretching your finger might cause it to roll off the larger hole. It's not uncommon for the thumbs to shift and leak air as well until you get the hang of it. Check your pitch against a tuner at first, to make sure you are using the right amount of breath. You can also compare the pitch with high B. If the pitch is too high, check for air leakage first, then adjust your breath. Remember to keep your fingers as flat as possible, since the pads of your fingers do the best job of sealing the holes.

The other subhole allows you to get two more notes.

This time, your left middle finger slides to cover the subhole. Check again to make sure you have a good seal over both holes; blow gently, testing with a tuner. Just like when you learned B♭ earlier, this note will be especially useful in keys like F major and D minor, where a B♭ is required.

The following etude alternates low B♭ and middle C.

Put all three notes to use now. These measures use C, B♮, and B♭.

In music, a natural sign (♮) cancels a flat or a sharp, either from a preceding note or from the key signature.

Make sure your fingers have finished sliding over the holes before you start to play the next note.

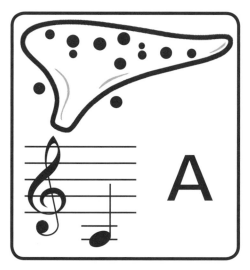

To play A, both fingers slide to cover the subholes, so now you are covering all 12 holes with your ten fingers. This is the most difficult note to play in tune. Check for air leakage; use a tuner to check your intonation again.

Use this next exercise to practice low A.

We want to practice the subholes some more, so let's play a song in A minor. A minor uses the same notes as C major, so B is natural for this lullaby.

ALL THE PRETTY LITTLE HORSES

American Folksong

"Shalom Chaverim" is in E minor, a key we first encountered on page 49.

SHALOM CHAVERIM

Traditional Israeli Folksong

"Danny Boy" is a well-loved ballad set to an Irish tune known as "Londonderry Air."

DANNY BOY

Traditional Irish Melody
"Londonderry Air"

Now you are well on your way to playing lots of music. Having three more low notes gives you more range and makes it easier to play in different keys.

Transverse 12-Hole Alto C Fingering Chart

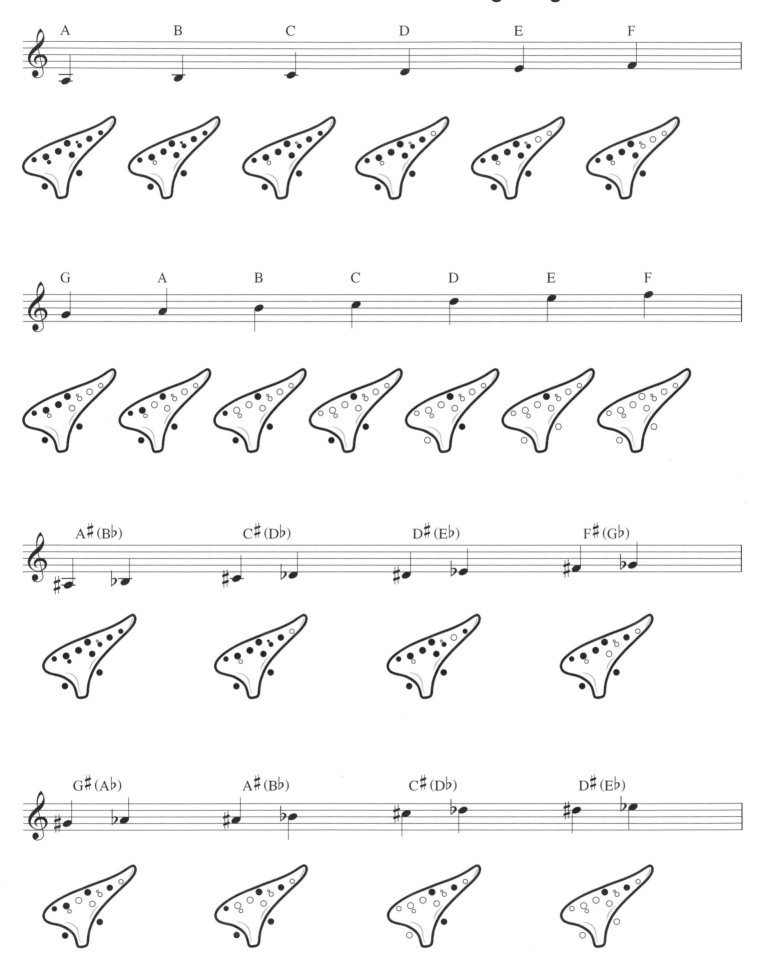

For an Alto C ocarina, the actual pitch of the notes is one octave higher than the notes written on the page.

PRACTICE SCALES

At this point, it's a good idea to practice the scales we know so far. Then, by learning more sharps and flats on the fingering chart, it will be possible to play more scales and more music.

C MAJOR

F MAJOR

G MAJOR

D MAJOR

To play in this key, F and C are both sharp. Check the fingering chart for how to play low C♯, and also high C♯. For now, the sharp sign is by the note.

The following measures call for low C♯.

D major is the key signature now. As you play the next exercise, make sure you finger F♯ and C♯.

B♭ MAJOR

To play in this key, B and E are both flat. Check the fingering chart for how to play low E♭, and also high E♭. For now, the flat sign is by the note.

Set your sights on this exercise. It calls for high E♭.

B♭ major is the key signature now. As you practice the next exercise, remember to play B♭ and E♭.

Pendant Six-Hole Fingering Chart

The pendant is a diatonic instrument, meaning you cannot easily play all the sharps and flats. Because your pendant may not be concert tuned, the notes you play on your pendant may not sound exactly like the notes on the page. Because you can play the ocarina as a transposing instrument, you can still use the C fingerings to play a diatonic scale in the key is which your ocarina is tuned.

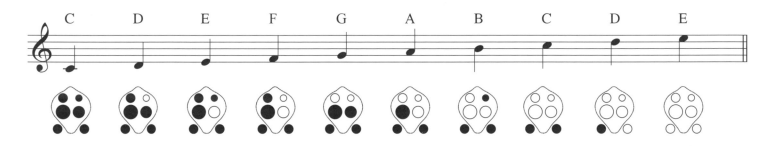

Additionally, you might enjoy experimenting with these easy scales. While scales limit your available notes, if you stick to the notes within the scale, you can create melodies more easily, since these notes naturally sound good together.

PENTATONIC

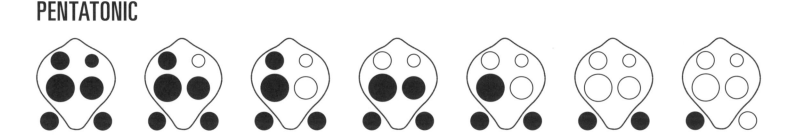

MINOR

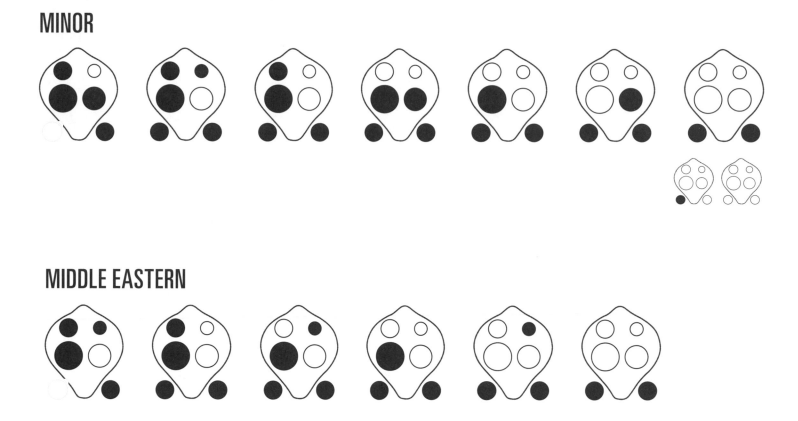

MIDDLE EASTERN

Music can be a great way of expressing yourself. When you find the melodies that express what you want to say, don't hesitate to share them. I hope you enjoy your musical journey with the ocarina!

ABOUT THE AUTHOR

Cris Gale is foremost an ocarina soloist, but is also an ocarina designer, educator, and popularist. Like so many others, Cris initially learned about the ocarina from Nintendo's *The Legend of Zelda: Ocarina of Time*. While she was originally trained in the flute, the magical sound of the ocarina was irresistible, and in 1999 the ocarina became her primary instrument.

Frequently invited to perform at international festivals, Cris works with both international and domestic cultural interchange organizations – not only to advance the ocarina, but also to increase cultural understanding through music. She co-headlined the USA-Japan Goodwill Concert at Carnegie Hall, and is the founder and president of the United States Ocarina Association. As an ocarina ambassador, Cris gives educational presentations at schools, clubs, conventions, and festivals, including the United States Ocarina Festival, which she organizes.

If you'd like to learn more about Cris, or are interested in ocarina lessons, please visit her website at *http://CrisGale.com*.